God Was Always There 2020

Teresa Ann Coleman

TRILOGY CHRISTIAN PUBLISHERS
Tustin, CA

Trilogy Christian Publishers
A Wholly Owned Subsidiary of Trinity Broadcasting Network
2442 Michelle Drive
Tustin, CA 92780

God Was Always There 2020

Copyright © 2021 by Teresa Ann Coleman

Scripture quotations marked NIV are taken from the Holy Bible, New International Version®, NIV®. Copyright © 1973, 1978, 1984, 2011 by Biblica, Inc.TM Used by permission of Zondervan. All rights reserved worldwide. www.zondervan.com. The "NIV" and "New International Version" are trademarks registered in the United States Patent and Trademark Office by Biblica, Inc.TM. Scripture quotations marked NKJV are taken from the New King James Version®. Copyright © 1982 by Thomas Nelson. Used by permission. All rights reserved. Scripture quotations marked TLB are taken from The Living Bible copyright © 1971. Used by permission of Tyndale House Publishers, a Division of Tyndale House Ministries, Carol Stream, Illinois 60188. All rights reserved.

Clip art by freepik.com.

Hand drawn art by Tattoo Artist, Jessie Returns jreturnstattoos@gmail.com.

No part of this book may be reproduced, stored in a retrieval system, or transmitted by any means without written permission from the author. All rights reserved. Printed in the USA.

Rights Department, 2442 Michelle Drive, Tustin, CA 92780.

Trilogy Christian Publishing/TBN and colophon are trademarks of Trinity Broadcasting Network.

For information about special discounts for bulk purchases, please contact Trilogy Christian Publishing.

Trilogy Disclaimer: The views and content expressed in this book are those of the author and may not necessarily reflect the views and doctrine of Trilogy Christian Publishing or the Trinity Broadcasting Network.

Manufactured in the United States of America

10 9 8 7 6 5 4 3 2 1

Library of Congress Cataloging-in-Publication Data is available.

ISBN: 978-1-63769-460-2

E-ISBN: 978-1-63769-461-9

"The writings from Teresa are a beautiful gift. Her writings have brought a perfect touch of encouragement to the beautiful families we serve, whether it's a time of needed encouragement as they are caring for their loved ones or a time of providing a source of comfort during their time of bereavement. The words she has chosen truly have sweetly saturated the hearts of many."

—Robin Teal, Volunteer Coordinator
Heart of Georgia Hospice

"The cards that Teresa gives to the Rescue Mission touches lives in so many ways. We hand her cards out to our donors at the Rescue Mission. They always leave with a smile and get to hear the name of our Lord and Savior, Jesus Christ! I don't think it gets any better than that!"

—Pat Chastain, CEO/President
Rescue Mission of Middle Georgia

Dedication

I dedicate this book to the memory of my late father and mother. My father, retired Army CSM, Kenneth L. Stevens Sr., served two tours in the Vietnam war and was a decorated soldier. War changes people and families. My father suffered from PTSD and ailments from agent orange. He continued to put one foot in front of the other each day. My father's passing in December 2020 weighs heavy on my heart. My mother, Frances Woodruff, was such a wonderful mom; she spent a lot of time being a single parent to us kids. My mother was the love that kept our family close together; she was a God-fearing woman. Now with my father, mother, and my sister Rhonda Carol in heaven, life has changed here on earth. Losing a loved one never gets easier—it gets harder. Love God, love people, and live your life according to God's purpose.

GOD WAS ALWAYS THERE 2020

You are *beautiful*.

TERESA ANN COLEMAN

Find your *fire*.

GOD WAS ALWAYS THERE 2020

"You are worthy..." —God

TERESA ANN COLEMAN

Keep your head up. God gives His hardest battles to His strongest soldiers.

"I can do all things through Christ who strengthens me."
(Philippians 4:13, NKJV)

TERESA ANN COLEMAN

You are going to make it. *Trust me.*

GOD WAS ALWAYS THERE 2020

Just give me Jesus!

TERESA ANN COLEMAN

"You are enough..." —God

Smile, Jesus loves you!

TERESA ANN COLEMAN

Jesus, help me!

Somedays, I wish I could just wake up and find this has all been a bad dream.

TERESA ANN COLEMAN

"Don't give up on God..." —**Faith**

Hope.
Once you choose hope, anything's possible.

TERESA ANN COLEMAN

"Before you speak—think!"
Is it—True
—Helpful
—Inspiring
—Necessary
—Kind
...**Love**...

Please comfort my heart. I have never felt this kind of pain. This pain pierces me deep within my soul. *It hurts, Lord!*

TERESA ANN COLEMAN

As I sit here with my loved one,
loving them so much and
afraid to step away
because I don't want to miss a thing.

God, please take away all the pain my loved one is feeling. Please have mercy on them, Lord. Please show me how to help make them comfortable. Maybe massage their hands, feet, or read them the Bible.

I never knew, truly knew how much I loved this beautiful soul until now. Lord, thank you for every second you have given me with them.

GOD WAS ALWAYS THERE 2020

Lord, please forgive me for the times I should have spent more time doing what they wanted to do.

TERESA ANN COLEMAN

"Lord, my life already feels so empty; I never knew what an impact one person could have on my soul…"

—Love

Tears flow down my face like a river. I know I heal from the flowing tears. Lord, help me, please. My heart is broken.

"Blessed are those who mourn, for they shall be comforted."

(Matthew 5:4, NKJV)

Lord, I am breathing, *but I don't feel alive.* Lord, this is the hardest thing I've ever gone through. Please help me, God.

Lord, please have mercy on me. I don't mean to be selfish, Lord, but I can't picture life without them. I can hardly breathe, Lord.

Lord, please help me be the best loved one I can be. Please be with me as I stay by their side. *Give me strength as I kiss them goodbye.* XOXOXO

God, please be with me and my precious family. No one can fill the shoes of this blessed soul. They were unique, special, and loved.

Isaiah 40:31 (NKJV)
God, please give them the biggest set of wings you have. They always spoke of one day soaring with the eagles.

TERESA ANN COLEMAN

I loved my loved one with every fiber in my soul. Now I must let them go. *God, I don't want to let them go!*

Time is passing fast now. God, before I know it, they will be in your arms. I am going to miss them, but I know they are with you!

"Everything has its time." "To everything there is a season, a time for every purpose under heaven: A time to be born, and a time to die."

(Ecclesiastes 3:1-2, NKJV)

Please forgive me for the times I passed judgment on my loved one. I know now they were doing their best. *God bless them.*

"The Lord is close to the brokenhearted and saves those who are crushed in spirit."

(Psalm 34:18, NIV)

Lord, will I ever be normal again? My heart is in a thousand pieces right now. Please help me; I am so scared and lonely.

Psalm 91:4 (NIV)
Lord, please let me find peaceful shelter within your wings. Please cover me with your feathers.

Lord, please be with me as I go to sleep each night. The nighttime seems to be the loneliest. Please comfort me, O Lord.

"Do not fear, for I am with you; Do not be afraid, for I am your God. I will strengthen you; I will help you; I will hold onto you with my righteous right hand."

(Isaiah 41:10, NIV)

Life is so full of surprises. But when life comes to a close, we usually would not change one surprise. *God is good, God is love.*

When you share crazy stories of your loved one, *laugh until you cry*. Some stories cannot be made up; truth is crazier than fiction.

Lord, I have never been alone in this big world by myself; *what if* I can't do this, Lord?

"Trust in the Lord with all your heart and lean not on your own understanding; In all your ways acknowledge Him, and He shall direct your paths."

(Proverbs 3:5-6, NKJV)

"Do not neglect to show hospitality to strangers, for by this some have entertained angels without knowing it." (Hebrews 13:2, TLB)

TERESA ANN COLEMAN

"You are loved...XOXO..." —God

God, I know my loved one is coming home with you. Lord, please tell me what I need to say to be *saved* as well. God, please show me how to *pray!*

TERESA ANN COLEMAN

"Jesus said to him, 'I am the way, the truth, and the life. No one comes to the Father except through Me.'"

(John 14:6, NKJV)

"If you confess with your mouth that Jesus is Lord and believe in your heart that God raised Him from the dead, you will be saved. For with the heart, one believes and is justified, and with the mouth one confesses and is saved."

(Romans 10:9-10, ESV)

This, then, is how you should pray: "Our Father in heaven, hallowed be your name, your kingdom come, your will be done on earth as it is in heaven. Give us today our daily bread. Forgive us our debts, as we also have forgiven our debtors. And lead us not into temptation but deliver us from the evil one."

(Matthew 6:9-13, NIV)

"Then Peter said to them, 'Repent and let every one of you be baptized in the name of Jesus Christ for the remission of sins; and you shall receive the gift of the Holy Spirit.'"

(Acts 2:38, NKJV)

TERESA ANN COLEMAN

If you repent and believe in Jesus Christ, your name is written in the Lamb's book of life.

Lord, I need you in my life—every day, every hour, every minute, every second. God, I need you badly. Please, Lord, have *mercy* on me.

"Have I not commanded you? Be strong and courageous. Do not be terrified; Do not be discouraged, for the Lord your God will be with you wherever you go."

(Joshua 1:9, NIV)

GOD WAS ALWAYS THERE 2020

Lord, please hold my hand as you hold their hand. Please don't let one moment pass that they were not held.

TERESA ANN COLEMAN

"May *love* be what you remember most..." —God

Always pray to have eyes that see the best in people, a heart that forgives the worst, a mind that forgets the bad, and a soul that never loses faith in God.

TERESA ANN COLEMAN

The day I had to come home without you, my heart was in a million pieces. I just wanted to disappear...*I love and miss you so much!*

Tell your heart to beat again!

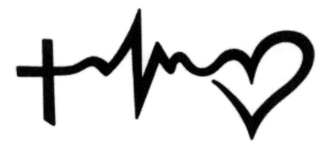

Sometimes *your mind* needs more time to accept what *your heart* already knows.

Time helps to heal our wounds. Time gives you a chance to grow stronger. Miss your loved one but never quit living your purpose.

TERESA ANN COLEMAN

Remember, life is lived one day at a time...**Just breathe**...

Lord, please help me handle the new stress I have in my life. Everything seems to easily overwhelm me. I get overwhelmed so much I just want to lock myself in my house and hide. God, I am really broken!

God, please help me learn my new identity as my role in life has changed. Help me accept and embrace the new me. Help me love myself.

When our loved ones pass on—just remember they are safe and in God's care. Your loved one wants you to continue your journey.

TERESA ANN COLEMAN

Everyone has a story of their loss, but they are not me. This loss feels bigger than I can handle. Lord, please give me strength.

GOD WAS ALWAYS THERE 2020

Lord, please help me to remember the good times we shared. Laughing over the silliest things. Help me to laugh again.

TERESA ANN COLEMAN

Good friends help you find important things when you
have lost them:
> your smile,
> your hope,
> and your courage.

Keep it really simple!

Forgive yourself.

Lord, please help me get out of this *"big black hole"* I have fallen into. I need you now, Lord. Please don't fail me.

TERESA ANN COLEMAN

Lord, please help me put these emotions into words.

Today was the worst day ever! Your cemetery name marker came in. It finalized the fact you are gone from my sight. You are not coming back to our home...*I love you!!!*

Lord, I never knew I could cry so much. With every passing day comes another holiday. I never realized we had so many holidays. That doesn't even count our special days! I am broken, Lord.

So many people loved you! The phone rings; oh how I wish it were you calling me just one more time. I miss hearing your voice.

It's okay to *not be okay, but always remember* you are loved!

GOD WAS ALWAYS THERE 2020

The darker the night, *the brighter the stars.*

TERESA ANN COLEMAN

One thing I found out is now that my loved one is safe, happy, and in heaven, I speak to them more now than ever before. Weird, huh?

Lord, I am going to miss so many little things about my loved one. The way they smell—oh, I can close my eyes and smell their *scent* right now!

TERESA ANN COLEMAN

I am really going to miss their silly laugh. Their laugh would get the whole room laughing, not to mention their beautiful smile.

Somedays, I wake up crying, and I cry all day long. If you ask me why I just cry that much more...Let your tears flow.

TERESA ANN COLEMAN

Isaiah 46:4 (NIV)
"I will carry you...Love, God."

Lord, please help me find my focus. I feel so confused even over the smallest decision. Lord, I can't think straight. I feel like I am going crazy! I feel like I walk in circles all day long—getting nowhere.

"Be still and know that I am God."

(Psalm 46:10, NKJV)

Serenity Prayer

God, grant me the serenity to accept the things I cannot change, the courage to change the things I can, and the wisdom to know the difference. Amen.

Romans 8:28 (NIV)
Even when you do not see it, God is working things out for your good.

Lord, I can only imagine what they must be seeing now. Your smiling face shining upon them, saying, "My child, well done."

Lord, I pray heaven is not too far away. Please let my loved ones come visit me in my dreams. I miss them so much, Lord.

Grief never ends, but it changes. It's a passage, not a place to stay. Grief is not a sign of weakness nor a lack of faith. It is the price of *love*...

The moment you are ready to quit is usually the moment right before a miracle happens!
Don't give up!!!

"We need to talk…Love, God."

Be sure to continue telling the stories and speaking of your loved ones—it keeps their memory alive.

"Come, my beloved child, and walk with me. Share your feelings and emotions with me. Talk to me heart to heart, let me help you. You are never alone; *lean on me*. I love you!"

—God

"But those who wait on the Lord shall renew their strength; they shall mount up with wings like eagles, they shall run and not be weary, they shall walk and not faint."

(Isaiah 40:31, NKJV)

Lord, the loss of my loved one has unexpectedly opened wounds from my past losses of other loved ones.

TERESA ANN COLEMAN

Lord, I feel like I have walls crashing down on me. It's hard to breathe; my body just wants to hold my breath. Please help me catch my breath! God, I hurt from head to toe.

God, please help me grow stronger from all of this. I thought things got easier as you get older—I just realized I was *wrong*.

TERESA ANN COLEMAN

Life does not get easier...you get stronger.

Do not take your eyes off of Jesus...Stay focused...your life depends on Him.

Isaiah 43:2 (NIV)
When you go through deep waters,
I will be with you, God.

"For God so loved the world that He gave His only begotten Son, that whoever believes in Him should not perish but have everlasting life."

(John 3:16, NKJV)

TERESA ANN COLEMAN

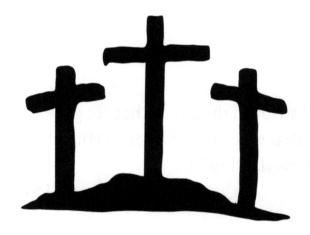

"I am still in control...Love, God."

Jesus' name and blood have power.

God hears us pray even when we can't find the words—tears.

Don't just be kind to others, be kind to yourself.

TERESA ANN COLEMAN

Pray for each other. "For where two or three are gathered together in My name, I am there in the midst of them." (Matthew 18: 20, NKJV)

People may not remember what you say, but they never forget how you treated them!

TERESA ANN COLEMAN

God's love letter to me:
B—basic
I—instructions
B—before
L—leaving
E—earth

Dear Lord, thank you for being my heavenly Father. Thank you for loving me unconditionally. Thank you for all the blessings you have given me. I ask you, Lord, to be with me as I go through this mourning process. Please help me to read your Word—the Bible—daily. Help me build the closest relationship with You; I love You, Lord.
In Jesus Christ's name, Amen.

Hotline Help Numbers

- 911
- Suicide Hotline—800-273-8255
- Addiction Hotline—800-662-4357
- TBN TV Ministry and Prayer—714-731-1000
- K-Love Christian Music, Ministry and Prayer—800-525-5683
- DAYSTAR TV Ministry and Prayer—800-329-0029
- Focus On The Family—800-232-6459
- Hospice Grief Counseling—search for hospice in your area.
- CTN-WGNM TV Ministry and Prayer—478-474-3986
- Pet Help line—952-435-7738

GOD WAS ALWAYS THERE 2020

Teresa's Favorite Songs

The Old Rugged Cross—Alabama
How Great Thou Art—Elvis Presley
Amazing Grace—John Newton
Bridge Over Troubled Water—Jim Nabors
In the Garden—Alan Jackson
When We Fall Apart—Ryan Stevenson
I Can Only Imagine—Mercy Me
God's Not Done with You—Tauren Wells
Who You Are to Me—Chris Tomlin
God Only Knows—For King & Country
Tell Your Heart to Beat Again—Danny Gokey
Just Be Held—Casting Crowns
Dancing in the Sky—Dani and Lizzy
There was Jesus—Zach Williams and Dolly Parton
God Bless the USA—Lee Greenwood
Unforgettable—Natalie Cole and Nat King Cole Duet

"Just when the caterpillar thought the world was over, it became a butterfly."

Proverb

CPSIA information can be obtained
at www.ICGtesting.com
Printed in the USA
LVHW062004101121
703002LV00012B/275